Unlike
Almost Everything Else
In The Universe

by
Howard Seeman, Ph.D.

Bloomington, IN Milton Keynes, UK
authorHOUSE

AuthorHouse™
1663 Liberty Drive, Suite 200
Bloomington, IN 47403
www.authorhouse.com
Phone: 1-800-839-8640

First published by AuthorHouse 6/20/2007

ISBN: 978-1-4259-9576-8 (sc)

Library of Congress Control Number: 2007903121

Printed in the United States of America
Bloomington, Indiana

This book is printed on acid-free paper.

To my wonderful daughter
Jaimelyn
to whom I gave
life
and by having her to love
gives it <u>more</u> back to me.

Contents

Foreword

I met Howard Seeman over twenty years ago when we were in a poetry group together. Most of us were sure about our sculpted words - definite, convinced despite the agony or disappointments they had sprung from. Not Howard. Howard [at a sunrise] was writing things like, "I don't remember any appointment here/ Am I supposed to do something?" While we were pinning down the chloroformed butterflies and beetles of our lives, he was out playing with them and engaging them in open conversation. He was the genuine explorer.

Howard is aware of each moment and *in it* slowly, deeply. And the truth found in our mortality, in all its finite fragility, flutters his concerns the most. Whether he is conversing with the sunset or throwing his daughter up into the sky, he is asking questions and unlike so many of us, waiting around for the answers. And the answers are the exciting part of these poems, poems that make us read closely and want to return to them again. "The sun's rise was g l o r i o u s l y / as it should be. / And I was ordinary / as I should be."

And what are some of his discoveries? Well: "I was alone in my life here / to feel my life alone" and "to decide who I had become." From a childhood of pain springs a grown lover of people, bays, cliffs, oceans, old men, long walks, a dying friend, children, poems, choices. Some of his poems are very, very funny. Some not, but they are still grabbers of our hearts, speakers to the center of the very cores we want so much to define and accept. They show us a man who has become very, very brave just by throwing out greetings, dares and invitations, then waiting patiently: "Since I have been lit up for such a short time / what should I reach out my hands for?" And the answers often are wonderful finds that are quietly thrilling: "I can lose many events / and be alone long / and there remains for me, a me."

Carmen Mason, *Poet; R.P. Creative Writing Instructor, New School University, New York City; awarded Poet's House, and NYC Bd. of Ed., Grace A. Croff Memorial Prizes for Poetry.*

Preface

I was an accident. My parents did not intend to create me. I am alive only due to their need for each other and their sexual attraction. When my mother, only nineteen, realized she was pregnant, with fear of little or no parental support, she, with the assistance of my father, tried to abort me by jumping off tables, running in her ninth month, and taking hot baths.

I was barely born, premature, turned the wrong way, bleeding, and delivered by forceps.

I am extremely lucky, and privileged to have the unique, awesome experience
(unlike almost everything else in the universe)
of *being alive.*

So are you.

Howard Seeman

Introduction

Emily, who has just died and wants to go back to her 12th birthday, says, as she watches people at her own funeral: "It goes too fast. Live people don't understand."

Our Town by Thornton Wilder

Come on, come on, the grand parade is passing right outside your door.

Suggested by the song: "The Big Parade" recorded by Jane Olivor

I found one of my best teachers on the boardwalk at Coney Island. He was homeless, and I sat on the edge of the wooden supports with him, dangling our feet over the side. He told me about his schedule, panhandling, sleeping in a church....

But he told me that most of the time he stayed on the boardwalk, facing the water.... And I asked him why. Why didn't he go to one of the shelters? Why didn't he check himself into the hospital for detox?

And he just stared out at the ocean and said, "Look at the view, young lady. Look at the view."

And every day, in some little way, I try to do what he said. I try to look at the view.

Unofficially attributed to Anna Quindlen at: http://www.ecst.csuchico.edu/~amarth/humor/commencement.html

Unlike Almost Everything Else In The Universe

There is not much you can do with this life

You can build a sand castle at the beach,
the waves will knock it down.

You can make a snow man,
it will melt.

You can work on a career,
it will end.

There is not much you can do with this life,
but talk about it.

You can publish a novel,
eventually it will not be read.

You can carve a sculpture in stone,
eventually it will fall apart.

You can make dear friends,
they will die.

There is not much you can do with this life,
but talk about it.

You can be world famous,
eventually you will be forgotten.

You can make your own children,
they will die.

There is not much you can do with this life,
but talk about it.

You can talk about it.

You can realize you are alive,
unlike all the tables and chairs in this room,
unlike the tall buildings,
or even the planets,
and all the stars;
unlike almost everything else in the universe.

You can feel you are being-in-the-world.

You can feel you are awake.

You can hear, smell and feel,
even what's behind you.

You can see and feel and hear and taste and touch
all the things that cannot see or feel, or hear, or taste, or touch.

You can feel like crying from joy,
like raging,
like caring, hoping, hating, loving, craving;
feel sad, mad, bad, glad, clad,
and had.

And you can talk about it:

You can wrap your tongue around it,
wrangle it with the muscles in your mouth,
and say it all,
out loud,
or onto large paper,
or buildings.

You can grab your hand around it,
make it into a fist,
and punch it out there.

You can spread your arms wide
and shout it out,
that you know.

And tell them.

There is not much you can do with this life,
but talk about it.

I

Not Realizing

I have been so busy

I have been so busy
taking care so many things
that I hardly hear the ocean.

I have been rushing to so many places
that I barely notice the stars.

As if fingers from the sky
    reach down onto
      my head and
        spin me
          like
            a
          top,

I seldom remember the ones I love
are frail.

I hurry their coffee,
wave good-bye as if they'll live forever,
and walk down the street
seldom noticing my own heart.

I'm mainly postpone

I'm mainly postpone.

I live as if it is all
'just around the corner';
and back it up with
remembering a false yesterday.

Living, really living,
I never get to.

I'd rather money,
or just accumulate,
than feel good about myself.

I'm mainly lazy-stupid.
I'm afraid to apply the breaks
and start down the right road.

I'm used to this way.

I am the me
behind the me I don't like,
watching him,
disliking him,
but don't yell him to get out of my seat.

I can't even get angry enough to change.

Sitting in a warm shit nest
is more comfortable than flying.

It's always: after I finish this.

I make New Year's resolutions
on every page of my appointment book.

I'm mainly postpone.

It's Just a Movie Anyway

I don't want to look out
        too far.

(Let me wrap my arms around myself.)

I'd rather stay in:
"just around the corner,"
"any day now..."

After all,
so I let some go by,
I've seen this.

...I mean,
it's just a movie anyway.

(I think I'll get some popcorn.)

What are you getting so excited about?

Howard, you're soon 30!
This is not a book.
It's you're life.
        (no, it's a book.)

Those aren't panavision scenes out there.
That's the real world.
        (but it looks like the movies.)

When you're dying and it blacks out,
it doesn't come on again.
        (ah, come on, this is probably the 3rd showing.)

This is the only life you'll ever have
        and then never, never.
Not even never,   NEVER!

        (come'on, what are you getting so excited about?)

He's that little dot down there

He's that little dot down there.
Right?
Crossing 3rd and 17th.

Oh, about thirty more years
(depends on what he does).

Well, he's <u>kinda</u> tried;
more convinced himself of it than done it.
Couldn't give up feeling grand.
That's been with him since about 5.

Shame.

Sometimes I've seen him laugh
like he could've loved
a million children.

But now even his anger's grown dim.
I feel bad,
                        shame,
well, ...

What? Yeah, O.K., I'm coming,
be right there.

Shame....

For another day

I ride my bike around the city
and notice that all the buds
are coming out.

I was able to not eat desserts
and lost 2lbs. this month.

I was able to do
10 push ups today, not just 8.

There are new babies in the park,
with optimistic mothers.

For another day,
I've convinced myself
that Death is nowhere.

Goes Round and Round in a Box

GOES ROUND AND ROUND IN A BOX
        about forty or fifty people
        (walking, legs hustling, crisscrossing in crowds)
        carrying their lunch, no heeds,
        hurry-moving, morning rush hour,
        just went by
AND THE MUSIC GOES
        and no one noticed a small piece of dust
        caught between the axle and the wheel-
        that it's spinning differently now.
ROUND AND ROUND IN A BOX, AND
        my uncle died, they tell me, 'cause a heart valve malfunc-
tioned,
        while he was laughing at dinner,
THE MUSIC GOES
        somewhere I forgot how I got from 12 years old to 31.
ROUND AND ROUND
        it's so hard to notice that your hands are wrinkling.
IN A BOX

One day in heaven

One day in heaven,

it's just about morning,

a nothing special day,

a bit dusty on the porch,

as two (they just got up) men

sit in their grass in their mouth rocking chairs,

just about morning, in heaven.

And one says:

"What's it you never did done?"

"I never really bothered to really push through

that stuffed cardboard hard to lift lazy

fiber glass insulation

between me and what I might do with my life.

I mean, most of the time,

I just sat there on the bus."

"Didn't you realize...?"

"Sure, but it's easier to live forever

until you die

and

it was harder to figure out than the crossword puzzle."

"Anyway,...

who knew?"

Kinda thankless

Sure, Dr. Glop-meyer,

let me show you our pancreas area.

Hi Jim.

He's our turbine operator;

keeps the pistons running smooth.

Jim's getting his pension soon.

As I was saying,

He's pretty tense nowadays;

lost often;

we have to work over time a lot.

Two days ago our committee brought up

the possibility of "heart attack;"

it was the blood and carburetor valves.

Today, you notice he's working better.

Yes we've enjoyed the work;

it's hard, kinda thankless.

Sure, I understand,

busy schedule.

Well, drop by again Dr. Glop-meyer.

Do you know your way out?

I wud da ant

I wuz da ant

on a baseball

walktin and thinktin

I wud da

powerfuldest inda wholt wurldt

when

rit in da midle a ma

wavin ma armzes and doin

great sings

some fuckinbitchbastard

smacks the baseball with

a BAT!

In the Bowling Alley

Bullshit man, my foot never touched the line.

It did so!

My foot never....

Ah, just go man. Go!

Hey Jerry. Did you hear about the guy who didn't talk
to his wife for months?

For <u>what</u>?

<u>For Months</u>. He was afraid to interrupt her.

Very funny.

Hank, give me some of that.

What?

That cake.

What?

That <u>cake</u> you fat asshole, that cake.

From the loud speaker in the bowling alley:
*"Ladies and gentlemen, can I have your attention please. The snack bar is open
for your enjoyment, and we suggest low fat foods. Thank you."*

Jerry!

What?

You don't really believe the Jets deserved that touch-down, do you?!

Leave me alone man, I don't get on planes anymore.

No you asshole, the football team.

Hank? Hank?

What?

You're up; you're on a spare.

He'll never make that.

Anybody got a quarter; I gotta call my wife.

"Attention Please! Reminder: Wednesday night is 'Two-for' night. If you bring a friend, your friend gets half off, and friends are very important."

How do you like that?

What?

I hit the side of the 3 pin and got the 6 pin with it!

Big deal.

Hank? How come you didn't bring Sam; I love it when he barks at the pins.

Hank?

Sam died, last week. We had to put him to sleep.

Really?

Phil, did you hear about Sam…?

Wow! Look at that ass!

Where?

Now, that's an ass!

Where?!

Forget it man. She wouldn't even go near you!

"Attention please. When you bring your scores up to the front desk, please do not cheat.
Cheating causes guilt, and low self-esteem".

I hope the fuck Schumer loses.

Loses what?

The election!

Shit man, you guys don't even know what's happening!

"Ladies and gentlemen, can I have your attention please. Play as many games as you wish, but remember: it is important to do in life what you really want to do, before you die.

I'm going home.

You just got here.

I'm going home.

What's the matter?

Nothing.

Hey Phil, Hanks going home.

Big deal, you're up, go, we haven't got all night.

Hank? Hank?

Jerry, will you sit the fuck down! You remind me of my old lady.

"Attention please. Trophies are on display at the front desk. However, remember: It is <u>not</u> true that the person who has the most things when he dies – wins."

What was that about winning?

What?

The loud speaker.

Hey are you going to bowl or what?

I feel bad Hank left.

Well feel bad <u>after</u> you go, your wasting time.

"Attention please. Please be careful; the lanes are slippery. Remember: After you die, your medical insurance only covers your wife and children, but not you."

Did you hear that?

I hear you stalling! Bowl for cry'n out loud!

**From the audience that is watching this play,
IN THE BOWLING ALLEY:**

Joe: "Hey, you bowling assholes! Don't you hear that loud-speaker?
   You're wasting your lives!"

Guy three rows behind Joe: "Hey, you idiot! Yeah, <u>you</u> in the second row.
What a ya yelling at the actors for?! What are you crazy?!
Don't you realize that this bowling-alley thing is just a play?"

Another guy in the audience: "YOU shut up! He has a right to yell at
the people in the play, it's a free country, and he's got a point about those
guys up there."

Another guy: "What are all you people crazy?! This is just a play!"

[The Bowling Alley on stage continues. The bowlers just keep bowling and do not hear the arguments going on in the audience. They are oblivious.]

"Attention please: Does anyone in the audience watching this play own a red Ford Mustang parked in the parking lot 2? You left your lights on, and you are not getting any younger."

Joe: "I'm leaving this play! Mary, let's go, this is stupid, now there's a ridiculous loud-speaker here in the audience; let's go!"

Mary: "No Joe, we paid a lot of money to see this play; let's at least see the ending."

"Ladies and Gentlemen: The theatre manager has decided that there will be a full refund to anyone in the audience who lives past 106. Please come to the office and fill out the Lived-Long Form."

Joe: "Mary, this loud speaker crap is getting on my nerves!"

Mary: "What Joe? Stop, you're yelling."

Joe: "What?!"

Mary: "You're YELLING!"

Joe: "I'm getting an usher; this is ridiculous!"

Mary: "Where are you going?"

Joe: "I'M GETTING AN USHER!"

Mary: "For what? Joe, JOE!"

Joe: "Excuse me, do you work here?"

Usher: "Yes."

Joe: "Can you please tell someone in the control booth to disconnect the dam loud speaker in this theater?

Usher: "Sir, theater loud speaker?"

Joe: "Yes, that loud speaker! It is driving me and all of us in the audience crazy!

Usher: "But, sir..."

Joe: "Call someone!!

Usher: "But, sir…"

Joe: Yes?!

Usher: "There is no loud speaker in this theatre; the whole P.A. system was removed a year ago."

Joe: "But, didn't you hear the loud speaker? No, not the one in the play, the one in this theater?"

Usher: "No, sorry sir, there is no loud speaker in this theater."

Guy in the audience: "Hey, Mr.! Sit down and go back to your seat and watch the play."

Joe: "Didn't you hear the loudspeaker here??

The usher points to the stage.

Joe: No, not the one in the play, the one here?"

Usher: "No."

Guy in the audience: "Hey, you. Sit down!"

Joe stares at the usher, then at the whole theater. Joe goes quiet. The usher keeps looking at Joe. Joe looks around the theatre for a long time, looking at all the people who are just watching the play.

II

Doing My Laundry

I've now tried

I've now tried :

   ocean

(remember on the bus "it would be wonderful")

Sun and

   resting, and

not resting, and

getting there on time,

   and being careful,

and not.

Is this all there is?

I feel like all I am is just:

DoingMyLaundry.

Dear world

Dear World:

Now just wait a minute.

Let's have some consideration.

I just finished, got oriented

to

set-off going, together: job, listen, dishes, laundry stuff…

<u>Now</u> what do you want from me?!

I didn't walk to the bus slow,

I left a tip,

been realizing that I gotta work right in there,
    (no lappsin' after Star Trek, I know)

but, Hey,

What the fuck is this some kind of game?!

My warmest regards,

P.S.

Horace still has a cold.
Aunt Em thinks Smokey is gonna have puppies.

I have become a place that nobody no longer visits

I have become a place
that nobody no longer visits;
where it is sunny
for no reason.

There are no longer any yearnings in the clouds,
nor some kind-nature
behind all the trees in the forest.

Birds have become
birds;
scenes,
too far away to care.

I now hear the quiet as only
quiet.

No matter where I look,
nothing calls to me.

I remember "living"
and how I said it with stern eyes;
but that's all gone now.

And the Earth
is just a moving rock
in nobody's space.

The Staff Meeting

The room is hushed;
they're not there yet.

The rug and the walls agree –
it will be some bout.

The outer door opens:
a rush of flame - the crowd roars.

Paul holds the door for Berta
(red sneakers on, no. 2, no owner;
Record: 5 and 7, known for
fire smile in her teeth)

They find chairs, each a corner,
all ready - scared – with acid smiles.

Howard: meek playing - dagger in right pocket.

Paul starts, sweet cream cover talk;
Berta grabs elbow;
Howard chops her across the neck.

All lean forward.
Paul strikes himself.
Berta saves.

Howard dives,
all on the floor – scream.

Give ups sounded - chairs back,
room quiet.

There are an awful lot of piddidles

There are an awful lot of piddidles
falling out of windows,
frayed rugs,
jars not on tight and…

Who knew?!
The dirt,
lost buttons…
and where did I put that phone number?
behind all those library of Congress
books and walls
and escalators and …

I mean,
I buttoned my shirt neat,
checked wallet, handkerchief, comb, pen,
tie knot is not tangled,
I turned the lights out,
locked the door,
got my list, checked the day.…

But still!
There's loose piddidles!

Rats in Brooklyn,
my hair's not straight.
There are pieces of buildings even falling down,
everyday.

I am still amazed

I am still amazed
that when I'm very sick
the walls around me,
windows, buildings, ...
go on
as if
I
or my hurt
don't matter.

Dear Howard

Dear Howard,

I'm coming back to get you.

You are probably (I see you) sitting
alone in a room,
it's dark and you've been waiting so long.

I'm sure you think I've forgotten you.

I almost did.
I'm sorry.
I've been unhappy too.
I got lost.

I ran very hard to keep up with all that good stuff you had,
but I got lost
in traffic,
among rewards, and girls, and tests, and my wallet, and calendars, and
lists.

I'm sorry.

Please wait a little longer.

I think I know where you are now,
and I've got some idea of how to bring you out
and take you with me,
and without getting lost again.

But it's going to be hard getting to you

because I'm also lost too when I don't have you,
like you feel without me.

But, I've got much more ideas of what's wrong,
if still not sure what's right.

We'll have fun when I get there.

Sorry, it's going to be hard,

much harder than we both thought.

We won't be able to be just spontaneous
(though we both want that happiness).

You see, Howard, it turns out that
the traffic out there
is more complicated than we thought:

Besides following our loves and coming from our insides,
we'll have to take care of each other,
not lie down when there's work to be done,
yet be able to lie down,
get angry when we're stepped on,
yet not at each other,
not feed ourselves the wrong food,
and keep friends more important than accomplishing.

And there's lots more.

I've got to go now.

I'm coming.

Don't worry.

I love you.

Howard

III

For Such a Short Time

Since I've been lit up for such a short time

Since I've been lit up for such a short time,
unlike all the other things in the universe,
what should I lean forward and stretch out my arms
to reach for?

Where should I turn my eyes?
What should I say while I can still speak?

Who should I stop and listen to
and feel that
they too are lit up for such a short time?

In a way,
I am always standing at the top of a cliff
over looking the ocean.

I am always dis-covering.

Light shines through me
then out:
lighting up everywhere and everything.

My door is always open.

Yet, off to the side,
I can hear the timer.

Eventually the latch will click
and the little space through which I look
will close.

Because I know this,
Because I know this,
I spread my arms wide,
pull in all the air I can,
and
dance in-the-glory-of-it-all.

The Bay

I kept watching
what we call
the bay,
going from high tide to low tide.

That is just the name we call it.

It is actually our world's pulse
exposed on the ocean;

the bottom gear
the earth moves on
as it tumbles through space.

As it throbs
it makes the lowest bass tone
humming deeply into space,
heard as far away as Pluto.

We hear it always,
but since it is always,
we do not notice it.

I was allowed
to walk on it.

It did its grand movements
every six hours
as it has done
for the last 12 billion years,
and with no attention to me.

I felt its time
and my time.

Under my bare feet
I could sense
the billions of fish
that were born and died there
and the ones now swimming
for their time.

This is my time.

Life goes as does the tide.
No bell rings
and only few markers.

My life is moving too fast

My life is moving too fast.
I realize each week that last week was wonderful.
Sure, I did the laundry, fixed the faucet, did my checkbook,

but I could've seen the stars,
felt the look of a child,
and noticed that my hands and feet move,
and everything else.

I realize each week, after that week is over,
that last week was wonderful.

My life is moving too fast.
I'm so busy driving that
I only see the towns from the side window.

When I step down,
there's an escalator under my feet.

I reach, as I go round,
for the brass ring... a little late;
it shined as it passed by.

Yet,
sometimes I lift my daughter into my arms,
and instead of
Ring Around the Rosy,
she just looks at me.

Then the car, the escalator, and the carousel stop,
and the brass ring is suddenly in my hand.

Then, there is no sound,
dying doesn't matter;
only my life to her life,
and she back to me.

Then slowly I shift her in my arms,
she reaches for my hair,
I pull back,
and the car begins to move, and the escalator, and the carousel.

My life is moving too fast.
I realize each week that last week was wonderful.

IV

Sunrise at the Cliffs

Sunrise at the Cliffs

When I was 23 years old, a woman I was dating invited me to Cape Cod with some friends that had a small cottage near a cliff that overlooked the ocean. She casually recommended that I get up early one morning to watch the sunrise: "It's a nice view from here."

So the next morning I got up alone at 5:30am and, wrapped in a blanket, sat down at the edge of the cliffs to see the sunrise.

I had never seen a sunrise.

I grew up in the Bronx, on a block. Up and down the street were just big apartment buildings and parked cars. All my life I had only seen the sun mid-afternoons peak out from behind high buildings, somewhat insignificant to my days growing up on my block.

Now, 5:45am, sitting wrapped in a blanket at the edge of a cliff, I saw my first sunrise.

Lynda Wismer

I don't understand this sunrise

I don't understand this sunrise
from this cliff.

I don't understand this parade-all-by-itself,
climbing;
that nothing lifts it
from such wide all-shoulders Ocean.

I don't understand this sunrise
from this   alone,   all the way over here.
How, Why it comes out of the ocean there,
        no sound?

How can there be
carburetors
and computers,
or how can I be
back hustling my alarm clock
and get voice mail
in a room with walls.

How is there such a roar I can't hear?
And why don't the waters there
where it comes
rise up, surge-bewondered,
and rush-in-a-crowd?

Why does not this cliff
explode now
and fly?

And this piddling-with-my-face-wind
stop
take on eyes
and gape?

Why does not this darkness of
light years of night sky, moon and stars
refuse
such a Universe Buzz Saw
burning,
rolling across?

Why am I suddenly afraid it may have eyes?
Why am I suddenly but a piece of cliff,
a non-member, lost midst
The Gathering of God's Control-Room?

I don't remember any appointment here.
Am I supposed to do something?

I don't understand.
I don't understand this sunrise.

The Sunrise Again

I came to see this almost 12 years ago.

Then, it was my first.

This time I took the road there
and went to see:

What now? How is it now?

(and the fear I knew that it was about me.)

This time I was bothered with
the cold wind,
being on time,
and trying to focus.

I had to tell myself:
this is it, be here.

I was, but differently.

It was a panoramic scene.
And, the ocean's waves below were friendly
(I'd been in them.)

The cliffs were not after me,
nor there a million years before me.
(they were)
but they were also there now;
with no evil in them
that might get me.

Then, I looked for it:

The Sun.

I was ready to be scared.

I was alone,
over fragilely the open ocean.

I was alone in my life here,
to feel my life alone.

I was about to see,
without any permission,
the birth of a star.

I was here to decide who I had become.

There was a kind of a drum roll,
but with cotton brushes.

It did shocking-wonder me how such a thing could do that.

But as it grabbed over the oceaned horizon,
far off there from my windy cliff,
(though it's light was amazing,
the source of all life)
It was OK

No thorn was in the light;
no fear did it put on me;

It was just doing its thing,
grandly.

I didn't need to hold onto myself for protection

It was the sun and me.

Each by ourselves.

And it didn't mind.

I watched it take off all it's clothes in front of me,
and its earth.

It was not angry at me.
(Giants never fear
thus never need be angry.)

The sun's rise was g l o r i o u s l y;
as it should be.
And I was ordinary,
as I should be.

I could've gotten into my car and left at any time
but I waited.

"Where's that grand scary part?"
I asked.

It never came.

It's just the sun.

It's just
me watching the sunrise,

and then back home.

I am at the cliffs again

I am at the cliffs again.

Fifteen years ago, I decided I was born here.

And now I'm at the cliffs again.

The only person it seems
that is still with me
through graduations,
remembering when I was thirteen,
and getting more serious about growing older
is me.

I'm at the cliffs again.

Much has changed inside me:
I tend to remember
the ocean
much less.

But, thankfully,
the ocean still looks at me,
knows I'm here –
though I only matter
as much as this grass matters,
or this cliff.

I'm at the cliffs again.

Much has died behind me;
a funeral parade I have slowly come by to be here.

No more Gail.
She's gone my dear cliffs;
don't know where,
and it doesn't matter much.
If I see her,
I'll send her your regards.

No more Gene
my dear cliffs.
He's gotten older and
plays ball to pretend young,
and joined the army again,
because he's lost and doesn't know where to find them.
And that's all he's been.
Sad, my dear cliffs.

No more parents as much.
They've grown much older
my dear cliffs,
and are living as children without children.
And are now coming back to each other,
and each other to themselves.
They are now in my photo album.

No more: "I don't know how," my dear cliffs.
I'm grown-up.
I know how most things now.
Waiting to learn for someone has to show me,
is over.
I'm now the one who shows;
I'm just about an uncle;
there are more little ones around me
than big ones.

I'm at the cliffs again.

I'm so glad you still recognize me.
I want you to know that I'll be coming back
to you when I'm 35,
and when I'm 40,
and when I'm old and turned 60.
And when I'm more going toward
being over
and sadder and slower,
and need help to get here.

I'll be coming here.
Keep a place for me.
I'll write my last to you, I promise.

And then you and they can throw it to the wind.
Kiss a wave goodbye to a ship,
and be off
to spend your next light years,
sunrises, ocean, travelers and all...
at the cliffs again.

At the Older Cliffs Again

For the first time,
since I've been coming here,
the cliffs look older.
I have just,
just now come here long enough to see
the cliffs look older.

That scares me.
I now can see for miles outside my rear view window.
I'm years and years and years old.
Things now have rusted memories on them.

The cliffs and the ocean
have got their heads turned away from me.
I'm only recognized by them from the side.
I'm no longer a novelty newcomer to show off to:
"It's only him again, let's just keep going...."

Across this cliff,
way out far in the ocean,
I hear it say:

"Howard, you've left us;
you're no longer a child of wander.
You've joined another circus.
You've turned your trailer camp into a home.
We move on to other towns,
but you stick the spike into the ground
and wave us goodbye down the road."

Yes, you are no longer
my great Walt Disney film.

You are no longer over my head
like some big Daddy.

You're more on my wall;
part of my home,
but at eye level.

At the Cliffs Again

No need any longer to capture
at the cliffs again.

They'll be here, and I can go elsewhere.

My home is now almost all inside me,
with Karen,
and the knowledge I can,
and can't be reduced to *can't*.

I no longer need to capture, go to, every year,
the *must* of at the cliffs again.

I can lie back in my living room,
or just watch Jaimelyn,
and can even die, if I have to,
at home.

Cliffs, we'll always be friends,
but I just may not call too often.

You are <u>here</u>.

V

Writing Poetry

I write poetry alone

I write poetry alone.

I write poetry because
ultimately,
I am, we are,
alone.

As if in solitary confinement
from my mortal cell
I write so that they will find these
when I am gone.

I write these to make contact
with the others
in their mortal cell.

I want you to know
that you are not alone.

I write poetry, not prose;
too many words
I have too little time.

I need to concentrate my words
to make them strong enough
to get through these walls.

This is important to do
in this short life.

I must find time
from fixing the car,
from going to the bank,
from even seeing friends.
[We too often talk
about baseball scores.]

I do not want it to be all over
before I, we, know it.

So, I come here
to be alone
to feel the compass of these formed words
to steer the more meaningful path.

Places that sing

Sometimes,
while I am going about living,
I come upon a place
that sings
like a song in my childhood
that reminds me of the ocean.

Suddenly, I am filled
with music.

At first,
I do not know where it comes from.

But I can feel
that somewhere here
I could mine for ore:
bright copper, silver or
gold wonders, wakings, or love;

that there is a spring here
rushing from the ground.

And, if I bend down,
listen carefully,
and write what it says…

magically,
comes this precious bird into my hand:

a poem.

It is such an intimate creation

It is such an

intimate creation

for me

to carefully take hold of

what is inside of me,

and form it for you;

and then raise it up to you,

outside of me

(as I balance in this emptiness between you and me)

holding it open,

like an unclothed statue

in the palm of my hand.

Like how I feel about:

my daughter,

or

my standing at the ocean at night alone.

When I write poetry

When I write poetry
I feel a little thrill
in the outlandish
audacious permission
to imprint for other people's attention
(for Pow!)
whatever (no matter what!)
the hell I want to.

It's a little like giving you a non-permission massage.

With abandon I throw out my feelings
like throwing out an entire deck of cards.

And what's even better, no one's looking.
I can do it at my desk, in the bathroom, on the train,
or while feigning dying.

And it's safe.
I can rip it up
spit on it
mount it in a treasure book
leave it
or make it a secret.

And it's real.
People look at it
react,
get affected.

And I can get my hands on it.
It keeps.
It's mine.
I take it out.
I know where it is,
where it grew;
and it knows me
well.

Sometimes my head is in the way of my feelings.
Sometimes my anger covers everything up.
Sometimes I'm too anxious or busy
to just notice
or to have a little me for me.

But, How wonderful!
There're always smoldering reminders:
poems.

That numbness when you tap

That numbness when you tap
on a plate-glass window
of an encased artifact
in a very large museum.

That not-feeling feeling
when you cross your eyes,
or roll them back
into your forehead.

That dead-for-a-second feeling
that comes
way back at the roof of your mouth
just before you yawn.

That feeling
when your alarm clock rings
in the middle of a dream
and waking:
everything feels
like looking thru a stuffed nose.

That feeling
when you can't find
anything
to write a poem about.

The Poet's Interim

The black velvet of sunset,
drowned-under by heaving earth,
calls to me
in my calloused night.

And I press my eyes against iced window,
heart against my eyes,
with a hunger like that brush for paint
as it crossed open-mouthed
Sistine ceiling;

I feel like
the desert waterwheel's
stop.

To write a poem

I reach for my sword
(I sneak my hand to the side
when no one is looking)
        to write a poem.

The world has its back turned
(perhaps caught in a conversation with mom and dad)
like I'm stealing candy
        to write a poem.

I pull my whole head down over it
and surround it with my shoulders
(as to protect it from those who might cheat from me)
to secretly masturbate
        to write a poem.

I let go of the controls of the surveillance panel
(the enemy could get me now)
and delicately (as if to remove a hair from my eye)
surgically pierce under my gut
to let my life blood bleed where it wants
(as if letting out my secret pet
who must be kept in the doghouse,
to have its run when mommy's not home)
        to write a poem.

And the blood runs out with gleeful freedom
(as genie from a bottle)
and feels its powers again,
up and away
(my poor bird gets so few times to fly out of her cage)
        to write a poem.

And she, my lover-poem, loves me.
She circles me.
Caresses me with her feathers.
Lets my stomach fly with her wings
from its chains,
whirls the world free of clocks and pens,

matters in spite of death
and lifts me
            off the earth.

VI

Realizing

There is not much you can do with this life

You can build a sand castle at the beach,
the waves will knock it down.

You can make a snow man,
it will melt.

You can work on a career,
it will end.

There is not much you can do with this life,
but talk about it.

You can publish a novel,
eventually it will not be read.

You can carve a sculpture in stone,
eventually it will fall apart.

You can make dear friends,
they will die.

There is not much you can do with this life,
but talk about it.

You can be world famous,
eventually you will be forgotten.

You can make your own children,
they will die.

There is not much you can do with this life,
but talk about it.

You can talk about it.

You can realize you are alive
unlike all the tables and chairs in this room,
unlike all the tall buildings
or even the planets
and all the stars;
unlike almost everything else in the universe.

You can feel you are being-in-the-world.

You can feel you are awake.

You can hear, smell and feel
even what's behind you.

You can see and feel and hear and taste and touch
all the things that cannot see or feel, or hear, or taste, or touch.

You can feel like crying from joy
like raging,
like caring, hoping, hating, loving, craving;
feel sad, mad, bad, glad, clad
and had.

And you can talk about it:

You can wrap your tongue around it,
wrangle it with muscles in your mouth,
and say it all
out loud
or onto large paper
or buildings.

You can grab your hand around it
make it into a fist
and punch it out there.

You can spread your arms wide
and shout it out
that you know.

You can see that they are all busy
trying to live forever
missing the parade right outside their door
not noticing the view,
not realizing that they are lit up
unlike almost everything else in the universe

and tell them.

And if they don't understand
or just keep forgetting,
you can love them.

Then, one day I realized...

For over 5 years
I have been taking walks down the Hudson River path.

I walk to the Winter Garden,
then to Wagner Park overlooking the Statue of Liberty.
Then, all the way back home.

About six miles a day,
usually five times a week.

One day
I noticed this woman going by me the other way jogging,
listening to headphones
and just looking ahead,
her eyes almost closed,
concentrating on what she was doing:
jogging alone.

What is amazing about this
is that on my next walk, I see her again.

Then, the next day, I see her again!
Going by me again.

I say to myself: "Boy, she is really into this."

What is amazing about this
is that I have now seen her every time I take my walks,
for over 5 years;
I always see her going by me.

Every time I see her,
I wonder:
Who is she?
Does she have a job?
Why is she so into doing this every day?
What is her life like?

Why is she doing this alone?
Is something bothering her?
Is she doing this for some important reason?
Is she a little weird?

Then, I realized....

I need to feel my place

I need to feel my place.
Not my place on the ladder
nor in my income
or in New York
or in what I need to learn.

I need to feel my place in my own life
and my life in its place.

Not for answers, or for making another list,
but just to have this place
this me
so I can w o n d e r i t a l l f o r a w h i l e.

For me.

Because I've forgotten.

And there really isn't
(when you get right down to it)

any
thing
else
to
know.

Spinning plates on long sticks

When I was young,
my mother took me
to see a show
where a man ran up and down the stage,
trying to save spinning plates on long sticks.

I was little then and didn't fully understand the spinning plates,
nor know that they were coming.

I just tried to ride my bike,
get Linda to like me
and run faster than Arden.

Sure, I would see the ocean
or Spring come
or a funeral
but right after it
just go get a soda.

But it seeped in:
when my gold fish died
when my snowman was gone
when I couldn't find that hole I dug at the beach.

I am now very busy
crossing out lists
fixing the car
and trying to get ahead.

I now see the spinning plates
wherever I go.

Man in the library

"Sir?"
The young librarian leans over the desk of the head librarian
a little scared to bother him,
yet too troubled not to ask again:
"Sir?
There's this man down in the stacks,
on sub-basement level 3,
sitting alone,
just writing there,
alone."

The head librarian looks up at the young woman,
seems to hear her very well
but says nothing;
and looks back down.

She now persists with some alarm:
"But he's down there all alone;
he doesn't even look up.
There must be a million books down there.
But, he's not reading any
nor even looking for one.
He's just sitting...."

The head librarian suddenly gets up
and begins to walk toward the elevator.
He says nothing.
The woman, startled by his abrupt move,
stops talking
and without understanding
follows him.

The elevator door opens.
The head librarian enters.
The woman follows.

There are 22 floors, a main floor, and 3 sub-basement levels.
The head librarian pushes the button for sub-basement level 3.

The elevator slides down slowly.

In the silence of the elevator,
the head librarian says nothing.
The young woman looks toward him for a long time to talk,
but, he stares straight ahead.

She finally gives up and looks away.

The elevator continues to slide.

It finally stops.
The door opens.

The stacks seem to be like trees in a forest,
books everywhere
in a silence like the emptiness of a closed stadium parking lot.

The head librarian walks straightaway
as if he knows exactly where this man is.
The woman follows.

Time goes by, they still walk.

Then, the head librarian turns left at Y310.67,
walks down a long row,
then suddenly slows,
stops,
and leans back on a shelf
and stares straight ahead.

The young woman looks in the direction of the head librarian's stare,
and then slowly brings her hand up
and places it, scared, over her mouth.

There is a man seated in a metal folding chair.
His head is down.
He is writing on paper in his lap.

He must have heard the librarian and the woman arrive,
yet he does not move from his writing.

He writes without any pause,
almost with a sense of desperation.

The woman looks to the head librarian,
but, he only looks at the man.
She hopes the head librarian will do something,
or at least look at what the man writes,
but, he seems to have no need to.

The man writes,
the head librarian continues to look on,
the whole library stands silent
like old trees in a canyon having seen this for thousands of years.

Finally, not able to stand it any longer,
the woman gathers her courage,
slowly steps three steps forward,
then three more,
leans over a shelf,
and looks through an opening between the books
to see what the man is writing:

...and now it seems
no matter how hard I peddle,
no more power comes;
as if the chains have slipped.

"Mom, I feel sick!"

"I'm sorry my darling,
but there's nothing I can do."

This one I cannot sell,
or leave
or drop.

I can no longer hold onto
my childhood secret that
I am forever.

I now realize that
rage only spins against the skid,
even long, long ago,
before religions.

I am realizing.
(like when I suddenly understood
that my father has to make the money he gives me.)

I now see old men with canes,
and see how I will enter that..

I was not ready for this.

My own body,
that I've grown to love,
(to bed, to sports, to prancing, to shining in the mirror)
is growing wounds I cannot heal.

"Mother, mother,
isn't there anything you can do?"

The man begins to cry.
The head librarian puts his head down
in silence for a few seconds
then turns and walks away.

The young woman reaches her hand out to stop him from going,
but the head librarian makes the turn
and begins the long walk to the elevator.

The young woman is scared.
She is becoming alone with the man writing in the chair.

The library surrounds her
like an old dead forest
alone in the night.

She looks away and closes her eyes.

She wants to apologize to the man,
but there's nothing she can say.

She runs to the elevator.

The day the story teller

"Here he comes!"
one of the kids shouted.

They dropped the ball
and ran from their game.

          (it was as if recess)

They gathered round him
for today's story.

"Today, I have a riddle for you children:

How is it that I was once 8 years old, like you,
small in the sunshine,
and now I can be fifty,
and tired, and routines, here in the park?"

The children did not say anything.

One started to giggle but was quickly hit in the side to shut up.

Then he didn't say anything anymore.

The children began to get scared.

("If a game, then we could move a little,
  anyone got a game?" - they thought)

He still didn't say anything.

Then, in the quiet, and in the childrens' wondering,

      he slowly, as if too heavy,
      lowered his head.

It suddenly got dark out.

Little Jimmy burst out crying and ran from the circle

(everyone knew to find his mommy)

and then little Sue, and then little Jackie, and then Bobby, and then Michael....

and we still are.

It is a scary realization

It is a scary realization
that when I am lying in bed
sick
the walls and ceiling
and all around me
do not care.

Clowns

As if they can no longer fly

from the reason for their fooling,

clowns die.

While, far away glass-eyed drunks drooling,

dizzily laugh at their own oblivious fooling.

Soft sighs, born to mourn

the tinted faces,

run to be mothered like cotton to lace.

But the harsh sounds that burst to curse

the barroom grounds

turn soft sighs cold.

Thus, clowns deaths are never told.

A certain smile comes over old people

A certain smile
comes over old people
when they see you again
after not having seen you for a long time.

We have all seen it.
We know it's not the usual smile.

Though we know how significant this look is
we never talk about it.

We just rush by it with a polite hello,
or talk quickly
and hope they don't directly say why
there is this *little joy* in seeing us again.

Then, sometimes, we run out of talking
that covers all this up;
we want to leave
and make some excuse to do so.

We make believe
we do not hear their need
and start to turn away.

As we begin to go
they usually shake our hand
and touch us in some way
that's a little stronger
than we want to be reminded.

Knowledge

"Knowledge" makes us feel upness

and it's because we can get our hands on

upness

better than we can get our hands on

opening

that we

knowledge – ourselves;

stomach out!

Dear God

Dear God:
Though you are probably not
and when we die
not even stars know;
(I call, but no one's home)

And though what we call
mother earth
is but hurtling rock;
(when planets pass by each other
there is no hello,
there is not even a wind).

And though our flowers to asteroids
are just dust to last Pluto
that really has no name;

Even though, even though
let me touch to something:
          some beautiful.

For one time once
just (even if illogical)
just, a little clear
care-tender:
"ah there's a little
     Beautiful."

You don't even have to wake for it.

It is such a ridiculous

It is such a ridiculous (I can almost hate myself)

thing

that someone has to tell you

or you must be laminated a movie in front of your face,

or brought pulled hand....

In order to realize that

life is not

things

(no matter how pleasurable, or right, or wrong, or terrible the crisis)

nor happenings

in which you are,

but,

just plain:

I lie myself down in the grass

(and it could be a city sidewalk)

inhale,

spread my arms,

and watch the clouds

make me.

Of all the things there is to be

Of all the things there is to be
      why not if I be
      a star-stuffer.

I'd roam the universe just a
      stuffing stars,
      a star stuffer.

For they must need something
      as they hang there so alone
      in space so empty.

I'm sure they could use something
      maybe a pound of cotton
      or soft velvet mush
      or perhaps foam
      [not the rubber-stuff]
      but ocean foam
    or baby foam
    or whipped cream foam.

Oh, to be a star-stuffer
      with only a bag full of stuff
      roaming from star to star.
      No tax forms, nor pension plan
      no tenure, nor budget.

      Just a star-stuffer.
      To just stuff,
      pat the star OK,
      and be on my way.

Do you know?

Do you know that I get feelings
in the bottom of my stomach?
That then go into my arms
and make me?

That I look out from
within here?

That I turn to look at something
because it *matters*
inside my blood and gut
that then goes into my fingers?

Do you know that I get
a worry- rush because
of a *time-thing* ?

That I want
from inside my chest,
that then goes into my muscles?

That when I bang my fist
it comes up
from way down in my feet?

Do you know this?

These happen to me all the time.

These wondrous events
have happened to me
all my life!

You too?

Sitting By The Ocean Trying To Be Great

Don't be (as a wave comes and hits the shore)
ridiculous.
You can't write
sitting by the ocean
trying to be great
writing by the ocean
about the ocean
trying to be great.

Don't be ridiculous.

It's wider than your eyes
sitting by the ocean trying to be great.

What are you crazy?

Do you know how many people stare
have spent days
books full of trying to write waves
sitting by the ocean trying to be great.

What are you kidding?

From Europe it tumbles
and tumbles into canyons
and is alone out there
and doesn't care, noticed or unnoticed
even in the night.

and nowhere does it have eyes
or arms
but all eyes and arms and all arms and eyes;
tumbling from Europe,
all at once
a not man's monster
doing it all (care or not) alone.

I'm no longer sitting by the ocean trying to be great.

It has scared me away.

I'm as all things to it.
I came from it, they came from it.
Somewhere we all remember.

I'm no longer sitting by the ocean trying to be great.

It has taken my talking away.

I'm a piece of cliff
or one day:
but one of the airs in the sky
or
(from Alpha Sentori)
no difference.

It's that
all of space and the ocean and the violence of the stars
are too loud to hear.

We   are   it   is   all   of   us   are   it
space, the ocean,
and I'm gone.

I'm certainly, no longer, certainly
ever sitting by the ocean trying to be great.

I Am A Musical Instrument

I sit in the waiting room
with my friend.
I am scared for him.
I look around and see all the other people
waiting.
I see a child.
I want to pet her head.
I take a deep breath.

I am a musical instrument.
Life plays me.

I ride my bike around the city.
I am along the East River.
I am at the South Street Seaport.
I watch people getting ice cream,
street artists performing for awed children.
The whole circle
has forgotten
that they will not live forever.
I know.

I am a musical instrument.
Life plays me.

My daughter argues with me.
I argue back.
I suddenly see that she is now a full person
I created.
I stop answering back.
"So Daddy?!"
"Nothing dear, nothing."
I lean back.

I am a musical instrument.
Life plays me.

I've Come Full Circle

I guess at this point,
there's nothing left to do
but to tell the old man
in the cottage up on the hill.

After all, he seems to know.

" Come in."

" I've come full circle."

He doesn't answer me.
He just looks at me,
relaxed, sitting there.

"But, I've come full circle!

I pained my way to get beyond being more than a child.
The childhood was no storybook;
I could have ended it all there.

But, in vengeance, I decided to try
to wake the Universe.

I wrote a monument at the start of my trail:

I shall return here with at least
a cup full of: this all makes sense.
I shall not go
and come and end,
as if nothing happened.

So, I went ahead,
lost in school things,
and Math things,
and survival things,
and not being liked things,
and TV things,
and doing without Mommy.

All along,
I always returned to my alone at night in bed
to remember my promise to myself.

The storm got thicker, with more side roads.

I lost the main road for the smaller ones:
job for the money,
for food,
for the movies,
for coping with alone,
for not feeling afraid,
for friends,
for pride,
for loss of weight,
for sex,
for feeling calmer,
for my desk things,
for the degree,
for Dad,
for marks,
for finishing,
for freedom,
for getting to what I really want to do.

I've come full circle.

I almost could have remained here,
and not gone ahead.

There's nothing ahead on the trail to bring back.

I have no cup for the monument.

I convinced myself that I'm clever.
I'm known by more people.
I have more names.
And, the sunrise is no longer new.

I'm tired.

But, there's nothing from the trail
I can take with me to dedicate to my promise.

It's:
you decide to live and survive,
you run after and join the tangles,
wrestle them,
you unknot some
and you're back to the simple string.

Now, it's a waste of time to make another knot,
to be in another tangle.

Try another monument?
Another promise?

But, if it's full circle,
what promise can there be?"

The old man listens.
Is he sad?

It seems he just lives.
He doesn't seem in pain from it.

Shall I just go old?
Is that all there is?

I cannot stay here.
This is his cottage, not mine.

"I've come full circle."

I notice he requires no apologies.

As

Like a soft glove smooths-sweeps over
rough suede and collects it calm
I am warming coming together.

As
slowly, with a bringing
as the meadows wave
as the leaves turn to the sun,
as,   as,   I am as.

The waves I watched in California
(where I ran away to)
have let go.

Learning to make friends is now:
friends.

Being a man is now
living as a man.

I can lose many events
and be alone long
and there remains for me, a me;

and, at least always
a home
with a porch out in front.

I feel as.

(as the forest grows)

VII

Jaimelyn

Dear Mom:

Dear Mom:

I have been allowed to create a little princess.
We've never done it before,
but it seems that we've done a perfect job.

And she shall spin like a crystal dancer in a glass.

We blew life into a space that had not been
and now
there shall be a dancer.

I will lift her
her arms raising high
and she will go from not realizing she is a child
to realizing she was a child.

And I will know all of this long before she
can even understand.

And by the time I can explain it to her
and she realizes....
I shall be
old
watching her realize
I made her feel like a little princess.

My daughter is so young yet

My daughter is so young yet,
so close to having just become alive
that her look at me with her eyes
is as if from the other side
where I was once
before alive.

She still bubbles with the
can't believe that she moves
that her hands and feet move
and everything else.

A bud has burst
in the dark universe again
like the flames from the sun
and this time
it's little Jaimelyn that's alive!

I watch her like I have often stared at a fire
burning and wrapping itself (and me)
around itself-myself
in an intimate quiet room, for hours.

I forget that I move too,
my hands and feet move
and everything else.

And then there's...

There's the stars at the beach at night.
There's the expanse of the Grand Canyon
at sunset.

There's the earth
seen from the surface of the moon.

And then, there's
sitting on a small mountain of rock
in Central Park
watching my daughter play on a slide below
while the entire St. Patrick's Day Parade goes by.

Stay up there!

Each time I lift her out of her crib:
there's that "stay up there!" feeling
as when you do your first throw
of your model airplane
that you carefully glued
and painted and held.

That "go!" you say as you let it go
from your hand
      hoping
as you kind of lift it with your breath,
as it goes no longer in your control,
as you bend forward,
hands on your knees:
      "stay up there, go, go, stay up there."

Each time as I watch her:
like blowing a bubble from my own breath
that then floats on its own air to freedom
that then looks back at me.

Now her own self
looking at me
looking at her.

Our fingers are going into each other
while she is still moving away.

(go, go, stay up there)

Saying: "Bye Bye"

Say, "bye bye" Jaimelyn;
      say, "bye bye."
She looks at me wondering, not knowing:
      what is this that's going to happen?

Say, "bye bye" Jaimelyn;
      say , "bye bye."

I let go of her hand, she wonders even more,
      now a little sad,
I say, "bye bye".
      I begin to leave;
          and now she knows.

She knows I will be gone.
That reaching out her hands does not bring me back;
that looking more, or even crying will not work..
      She knows.
      She swallows, she looks around
and goes for a toy.

Say "good bye" Jaimelyn.
"Bye, bye daddy, bye."
"Bye, Bye Jaimelyn."
I leave.

"Good bye, see you next week, Jaimelyn."
"Bye dad; I'll call you on Wednesday."

No one really told me about goodbye.

They never told me there would be many,
then much more.

They never told me that some would be final,
whether I liked it or not.

   (If they had, I would never have learned, "bye bye".)

Jaimelyn,
I'm sorry.
There is nothing I can do about it;
even your daddy has to

Say, "bye bye" Jaimelyn.

Sometimes, me and my daughter

Sometimes, me and my daughter
are tickling, wrestling,
play bite each other on the arms
(I bite the soles of her feet)
we giggle, laugh and yell.

Sometimes, I read her a story.
She's sitting on my lap
her back is to me
but I so softly
touch my lips against her cheek
or shoulders,
as I rise and fall the feelings in the words for her.

Sometimes, I say, "uppy, uppy"
and I lift her onto my shoulders
and carry her down the street.
I'm the throne.
I bounce as I walk her
and, I'm up there too.

But, sometimes
as we come out of one of these:
end the love-wrestle
close the book
or bring her down to me
we suddenly both go quiet.

We look way into each other's eyes
and we closely see each other.

Then she sees I'm her daddy
that my hair is graying
and that I can lift her less now.

I see her,
and me
and the horizon of the ocean.

Slowly her smile (or is it my smile)
smiles her smile;
we know
we hug
and we go back to the world.

The Statue of Alice in Wonderland

My child used to climb on
the statue of Alice in Wonderland.

I used to climb on
the statue of Alice in Wonderland
too.

Now, there are new children climbing.

I used to be one of those dads
watching my child
going in and out of Alice's friends.

These parents know:
You can't stay
up there forever.

"No," says the little girl,
"I want to stay up here...for the rest of my life."

It is sad that Alice
cannot really see the children;
her smile would be even wider.
Dinah would play with the children too.

How many of these children
come back to watch their children
climb on the statue of Alice in Wonderland?

My child used to climb
on the statue of Alice in Wonderland.

I used to climb
on the statue of Alice in Wonderland
too.

VIII

Being Close

The Choice

Maybe I should get married and have a family.
I would love, be loved
lift a child through this world
be intimately close and protecting
and make a circle-bond on this earth
in spite of all we die.

But a permanent relationship takes a lot of work
and children cry a lot
and cost a lot of money.

I'll get a dog.

It'll wag me an excited hello
play with me when I'm lonely
and lick my wounds.

But it will want to be walked
in the rain
pee on my carpet
and cost me a lot of dog food.

I'll get a bird.

So it can't wag its tail
but it can chirp
(hopefully at me)
and I can call it by its name.
It'll land on my shoulder
and we can talk
or at least I can.

But it will make feathers all over the house
and need its cage cleaned.

I'll get a plant.

No crying, no peeing
nor walk it
nor feathers.

It'll be pretty.
I can still talk to it
and all it needs is water.
Just Tuesday and Friday.
A neighbor can water it when I'm gone.
I'll ask her; she won't mind
I think.

Maybe I'll just get a painting.

It'll hang there nice
cover that crack
and be no trouble at all.

Just a cheap frame
something in blue
with a glass that doesn't   need   much   cleaning.

Maybe   I'll   just
             won't
                  get

                        anything.

Yet, how wonderful

I am locked inside here
with only these eyes
and only these ears.

I can only see what *I* see,
what *I* hear.

I can only taste with this tongue
only touch with these hands.

I have only the drive
of my hopes, and needs and cares.

Yet, how wonderful it is
that I can listen
to how everything is
to someone else's ears
someone else's eyes, tastes, and touch.

Everyone brings me more eyes and ears,
tastes and hands.
Everyone brings me more hopes and needs
and cares and wants.

All are messengers
come back to me
waiting here in my small place.

One comes now.
I listen.
What more can you bring me?

It's like:

It's like:
Have you ever had yellow sponge cake
soaked in sugary wine sauce
handed to you as you sit
at a beautifully decorated table
with everyone in your family
celebrating a home coming, or a loving wedding
and happy fiddle music is playing
and your uncle comes in the door
and everyone stops and joyously yells out his name
and lines up to hug him
and then everyone goes back to laughing and dancing...?
Have you?

Well, that's what it is like
to listen to someone you love
and be close to them.

I remember a night

I remember a night,
my daughter.

Well, you see,
there's not much that like
stays,
I mean lasts.

I mean, well, this night
all these people,
we were just like
really nothing, but
it may not sound important now
but, you see,
we were

friends.

I let touch me

When you or my life

I let touch me

(and oh so seldom)

am I able

to not talk.

And then I say things

(and see you know it)

which are so close,

I want to talk again.

And sadly do.

Then it all goes away,

and I'm back in the world

of words, buildings and pens.

I don't like being in someone's eyes

I don't like being in someone's eyes.
Their world rolls me around.

I don't like when my hand gets
a "reach" in it,
and I'm out of myself.

The sudden fear, like over a cliff....

My seams seem to split.

I'm afraid that even my arms will cry.

I want to pull back,

but,

it feels so flying to be out there
(in someone's eyes).

No muscles, or I,
or clocks, or my,
no why's, or what's,
   or this's, or that's.

just   someone's   eyes.

There is a time in being

There is a Time in Being much more inside us
than the clocks on our watches and walls
or pads and calendars.

But we'd (and I'd) rather be immersed
in the clock-times of our days.

Karen (as innocent as she works so hard)
and Bob and Helen,
are all in this Time of Being
but they choose not to know it.

I look at them midst their hurrying,
trying to be this or that
and see them as these lit creatures midst
Being
and love them.

I will miss them as they too die
and love them.

So glad we had this stage,
performed our little miss muffets together
and then
never again.

Home

"Many years ago…,"
"Stop! Now wait a minute, don't start like that."

Some men jumped back a little at the interruption.

It broke not only the story Orgon
was about to tell,
but broke the silence of the night there
in the dark
fire lit cave.

"You can't start like that.
This is a remembrance
we must make of when
we used to hide from noises behind trees and rocks,
before this cave."

Orgon slowly nodded almost a sacred understanding,
and then began again:

"We shall call this a *h o m e,*" he said.
"We shall call this place where we come
to lie down and need sleep,
home.

We shall greet it like our pet that comes to us to greet us;
it shall welcome us,
protect us with its big shoulder-walls
and we shall be safe here."

"Honey, look at that one with the little bay windows."

"Excuse me, do you have a house for sale that's
near the ocean?"

Near the ocean,
near a stream so we can get water,
near the high rocks so we can see the deer coming,
near the fallen trees so we can make a fire.

I go around the side of my house
open the cellar door
down the old wooden steps
grab the hammer in my tool box
up again to the front stairs
and I hammer, I fix, I hammer, I fix.

I take care of my house who takes care of me.
She is old, but she still greets me when I come home
and protects me.

"We shall make pictures on the walls to remember
the flood time,
and when the jackal tore Ren's leg.
We shall make it pretty where we sleep
make pictures on the cave walls
so others shall visit,
in this
home."

Humans

They, as a secret, know that they are going to die
and spend most of their lives trying not to.

Within this room
they reach in all directions
full of caring, need and worry.

Sometimes, their hands meet
just fumbling, sometimes holding.

And, sometimes when they stay,
they start to know each other.

Then they can see that they are in the same room.
They see in the other's eyes
the secret the other does not want to admit.
And then they love.
And then they love.

And then they both see that all of the others
are in the same room too.
Then
the room gets wider.

And then they clearly see all the others fumbling
and know that the best thing is…
to hold one another.

IX

The Last Down Hill of the Roller Coaster

Doing The Math

I am doing Math that I never did before.
I've never done this kind of Math in my entire life.

I read that the new World Trade Center
will be finished in about
ten years.

I stop whatever I'm doing.
I have to figure it out.

Will I see it?

I'm 62.
62+10 =72.

Probably: Yes.

I've never done this kind of Math before.

I was glad when I heard
they were building a new park.

I was excited that they are building
a space station.

But, when I heard about plans to land on Mars,
I felt sad.
I will never see it.

I walk by men working on the foundation of a building.
All the workers digging in,
noisy trucks, dust flying....

I keep walking by;
the building sounds fade.

Many of these have all happened before me.
And some, are now.
And some, I will never see.

I turn around
and walk back to the building again.

Once these workers were slaves building the Pyramids.

They are all gone now.

This is my time.

Now, the noise here is like
the last movement of a Great Symphony.
The waving of a great baton.
The acoustics are grand,
and I have a front row seat.

Suddenly everything is longer

Suddenly everything is longer
heavier and faster.

I lie back on my floor
to catch my breath
and notice that the fan on my ceiling
is turning at its usual speed
but it's now fast.
I am slower.

The blocks to the store
are now
three long blocks to the store.

My child
skipping down the block ahead of me
now makes me a little sad.

I'm no longer a member of that.
I see it all as a memory.

I reach out my hand to have it again,
but my grasp goes thru it
like a ghost
longing to be there
the way it used to be.

When I was eight years old

When I was eight years old,
I was sure I could fly
if I jumped off a roof
and did not get scared
and just kept believing
I would not fall.

Today, I don't even have the omnipotence
to not get fatter.

I am really now convinced that
no matter how hard I try
there are many, many things
I
(no matter how much I believe,
jump, want, think I can)
can't do.

I also did not talk like this when I was eight years old.

Many things now remind me of
looking out the rear window of a car:

My daughter is now where I once was.
Sometimes she looks at me as I will have been to her
when she no longer needs me.

When she turns away to go to play,
I see that
she is already
a sunset memory I will have.

I see the seasons change
and now remember
how easily it happens.

There are much fewer new things.

I see the beginnings of things
that I will not see finish.

Sometimes I catch myself
(with a fear that I quickly rush by)
that when I am planning,
it makes no sense to figure that far.

Next, I will have to accept
that it's not that I did not get enough sleep,
nor ate wrong,
or need more exercise.

Something is missing

It is now Thursday morning.

I step out of my building onto 8th Street,
my block for almost 35 years,
and start my usual walk down the street.
I look: something is missing.

Have they removed a tree?
Is there a sign missing?
Something up toward the sky?

I look in the stores as I go by.
They all seem a little empty of something.
The breakfast place I have gone to a hundred times,
has something gone?

I sit down to eat
and look out onto the street,
something is missing out there.
Even at my table.
Even in my hands.

I inhale and realize that it is:
My father died last Saturday.

There are people all around me,
but here in my space:
I am a little more alone.

I can feel:
"Nobody can die for you."

I am now the elder in my family,
an honor to be leaned on,
and an intimate holding of hands
fills my aloneness.

But, I also know that I am the *Next*.

Such: straightens my posture for the wind,
and widens my seeing.

Here comes the last downhill of the roller coaster.

I've been to the top of the mountain

I've been to the top of the mountain,
spread my arms,
looked all around,
and took it all in.

Now I no longer
feel the complaints
of the climb.

I am coming down now
slowly,
appreciating
all I've seen.

As I pass each old place,
I appreciate it more than
at the climb.

When I reach the bottom,
I will look back
and feel privileged
that I was even allowed to start,
look up,
and climb;

especially when
I come down
to the end.

Many years have gone by now

Many years have gone by now.
They are somewhat alone now.

The walls of their home
(from their child)
gently, like a wise old friend, smiles,

as they go about their
simple tasks now.

There is only mending now,
and giving to old friends still needing them.

The days are more quiet;
things are older.

And yet
far off,
persistent as the mountains' shoulders that cove their little home,

he still needs reassurance,
she still worries that
he may not accept her.

I wish we made it to checkers

We see each other, as I get off the train to meet him.
I yell, "Jerry!" [his real name, or what I called him, is DaniEL].

He yells, "Sam!"
[my real name is Howard, or Slim, or Fats, depending on the week].

We run toward each other
as other people around us watch.
But, we run right past each other,
still yelling: "Jerry!", "Sam!"

After about five minutes of this routine,
we slowly walk back to each other
and do our special handshake.

We could not just say, "hello".
After all, this is a reunion:
we haven't seen each other
for over 6 days!

Or, seldom, if it's been more than a week:

I ask, "How the hell are ya?"
He comes back: "Who the hell are you?!"

Then, he says, "I go first."
I say, "No, I got important things to tell you."
He says, "Big deal."
I say, "Who the hell are you"?!
He says, " Ok, 10 minutes, but then I get an hour."
I say, "Ok, you go first."

He starts, usually with tennis,
though I want to know
about his latest medical report.

I listen, and listen, with a lot of: Great!s.

I say, "Now, I go."
He doesn't say anything.
I say, "Ok, that means I go."

"What did Dr. Ahmed say about your latest cat scan?"
"That is a medical question."
"Yes, I need to ask 3 medical questions."
"You can ask only 2."

"Ok."
 I ask, and he let's me do more than 10;
and we talk about these for over an hour.

DaniEL and I have been very close friends for over 30 years.

We listen, we talk about serious problems,
silly problems, and we play, and play.

We used to just do Frisbee.
Then another year: bowling every Thursday.
Then, for years: racket ball, squash, tennis;
billiards was our last fun thing
[while we were really
always hugging each other].

Once after dinner and our usual catching up,
on the way to play,
I said: "You know, sooner or later we will be too old for tennis,
even billiards."
He says, "Next is golf."
I say, "I hope we make it to checkers."

I loved DaniEL.

Six months ago, after I helped him fight as hard as he could,
for over 2 years,
he died of cancer.

We loved each other very much.

I often want to feel him and see his face again.
So I do.

Then it hurts too much.
So, I don't.

DaniEL.

I wish we made it to checkers.

I Want to Die Well

I want to die well;

not just the last hour, or my last few days.

Hopefully, I have about 20 years to go.

I want to die well for my next 20 years.

I want to do this slow dying that we all must do,
well.

This is my last chance at
doing as much as I can
the wonder of being alive,
before I die.

This is my *real* Final Exam.

As I go,
I do not want to
pull down,
detract,
nor take away
anything from anybody.

Instead, I want to widen others,
leave red carpets wherever I go,
ease burdens,
leave light,
and remind them too:
to not take this wonder of being-alive
(unlike almost everything else in the universe)
for granted.

I want to understand everyone so well
that I can't be angry at them.

I want to leave an after-glow;
not a depression, or an anger, or a weight.

I want to go out like a burst of flame.

I do not want to complain.

I want to be proud of myself
every night I go sleep.

I want to be brave:
to feel <u>every</u> experience,
be it pain, fear, sadness....

I do not want to hold up my arm in front of me,
nor turn away
as the winds of these feelings come.

I want to honor this final descent
like the thrill in the last steep down hill of a roller coaster.

This is my last chance.

There is no more planning to live well.

It's now or never.

I want to die well.

Acknowledgments

I want to acknowledge the first poet I ever met: my father: Alex See-man - poet, song writer, inventor…, who had the wonderful courage to do the impractical - who was the pilot light that ignited what you now hold in your hand.

And my mother, Rosalind, who taught me endurance and loyalty by example, and, lucky for me, wanted a son who could play the piano.

I want to thank the longest and most beautiful poem I have ever worked on: my daughter, Jaimelyn, who is wonderful in many, many ways, and who has greatly widened my life.

And, my wife Karen, who has had the patience and loyalty to listen to more of my poems, for the longest time, than anyone, and who created with me my most beautiful poem.

I also want to thank:

Carmen Mason for her Foreword, her dear friendship, her astute and caring listening, and her excellent, honest editing suggestions.

Terri Castillo for her time and spiritual understanding in reviewing the manuscript.

Stephenie Hart for her proof reading / editing of the front and back pages of this manuscript.

All my teachers who encouraged and supported the creative writing process for me and for all their students.

Bob and Ellen Siroka, David Wallace, Jim Sacks, Mildred Schwartz and the late Gil Schloss for the emotional education which helped me mine these poems.

My dear friends and family, who, by allowing me to be close to them, enrich my life and give me strength.

And my dear friend, Steven Wilhelm, who keeps inspiring me to <u>not</u> write a poem like his: "I hate this trip!"

About the Author

Howard Seeman is Professor Emeritus, City University of New York, where he has taught educational psychology, group dynamics and human relations since 1970. He was also an individual and group psychotherapist for twenty years, earning his Ph.D. in philosophy and social psychology at the New School University, New York City.

A consultant to troubled schools and teachers, Prof. Seeman is the author of the book: <u>Preventing Classroom Discipline Problems; A Classroom Management Handbook</u> with a companion training Video/CD used in U.S. schools coast to coast, and in over thirty countries. He is certified in The Training of School Violence Prevention and Intervention and teaches an online course at: <u>www.ClassroomManagementOnline.com</u> .

Born in 1942, he has been writing poetry for over fifty years. He is a Certified Poetry Therapist, and a licensed English and Social Studies teacher, who taught literature and poetry in the New York City schools for six years. He also conducted poetry groups for twenty years, and his poetry has been published in many local journals. He is a frequently invited reader of his poetry at many bookstores, cafes and community art organizations.

Influenced by e. e. cummings, Seeman says that he tries "to honor how experiences honestly present themselves, rather than heeding the rules of language that can distort the poetic expression of these intimate, aliveexperiences."

Recently, Howard realized that his main regret would have been not to have published his poetry. So, now, no regrets. He says that he will feel successful with this book if he simply hears that readers feel like giving his poetry as gifts to loved ones.

Requests for discount copies of this book can be made by emailing the author at: <u>Hokaja@aol.com</u> He also welcomes your comments and is available for special readings of his work.

For copies of this book, go to:
http://www.AuthorHouse.com

Author/Discount sets of this book are available at:
http://www.panix.com/~pro-ed/poetry/

Printed in the United States
82632LV00003BA/370-378/A

9 781425 995768